# Cormorants at Dusk

# Cormorants at Dusk

Poems by

Cheryl Baldi

© 2024 Cheryl Baldi. All rights reserved.
This material may not be reproduced in any form, published, reprinted, recorded, performed, broadcast, rewritten, or redistributed without
the explicit permission of Cheryl Baldi.
All such actions are strictly prohibited by law.

Cover design by Shay Culligan

ISBN: 978-1-63980-565-5

Kelsay Books
502 South 1040 East, A-119
American Fork, Utah 84003
Kelsaybooks.com

In Memory, Cynthia Beshel

# Acknowledgments

Thank you to the editors of the following publications in which these poems first appeared, some in slightly different forms:

*Amethyst Review:* "Migration"
*Arts and Cultural Council of Bucks County:* "Ash, Snow"
*ONE ART: a journal of poetry:* "We Speak in Whispers," "Sisters,"
    "Night Lanterns," "The Day Falling to Pieces," "Afterlife"
*Philadelphia Stories:* "In the Golden Hour, Cormorants"
*Schuylkill Valley Journal:* "Fledging"

Many thanks to Julie Cooper-Fratrik and Marcia Pelletiere for their insights and help shaping these poems and this manuscript. I also am grateful to Chris Bursk, who left too soon, but whose decades of encouragement and spirit inform the work.

To the many writers in both the Bucks County and Warren Wilson communities, thank you for your friendship and support, and for your extraordinary poems and stories that delight, nourish, and edge me forward.

Special thanks to Karen Kelsay and her staff at Kelsay Books.

Finally, love and gratitude to my sister's children—Susan, Jon, Dave, and Jeff—who lived many of these poems, and whose courage and generosity in caring for their mother and sharing their grief were my inspiration.

To our fledglings: Joey, Matty, Ella, Addison, Josie; to Colin, Fiona, Lucy, Julia.

To Jenn, Meredith, Eliza and David, Christa.

And to Rob, thank you for your caring.

# Contents

Fledging ............................................................. 15

## 1 Night Lanterns

At First There Was No Air ............................. 19
It Begins .............................................................. 20
Not This ............................................................... 21
Alveoli .................................................................. 23
The Day Falling to Pieces ................................ 24
Witness ................................................................. 25
How to Ask .......................................................... 26
Sisters ................................................................... 27
Morphine Drip ................................................... 28
We Speak in Whispers ..................................... 29
Home Health Aide ............................................ 30
Snapper Blue ...................................................... 31
Physician, Father .............................................. 32
Obituary ............................................................... 33
Last Everything ................................................. 34
Night Lanterns ................................................... 35

## 2 Atlantic Flyway

Ash, Snow ........................................................... 39
Deep Freeze ........................................................ 40
Bloom ................................................................... 41
Atlantic Flyway ................................................. 42
Fogbow ................................................................ 43
Squall ................................................................... 44
Nocturne ............................................................. 45
Late Garden ........................................................ 46
Renewal ............................................................... 47
After Ebb Tide ................................................... 48
Vespers ................................................................ 49

## 3 Suddenly a Rush of Air

| | |
|---|---:|
| In the Golden Hour, Cormorants | 53 |
| Another Morning | 54 |
| Of Children | 55 |
| Here's the Thing | 56 |
| Against Evanescence | 57 |
| Migration | 58 |

## 4 Fledgling

| | |
|---|---:|
| The Newest One at Three | 61 |
| She's Going Out with the Tide | 62 |
| Afterlife | 63 |
| Hymn to the Gods | 64 |
| Sky Dance | 66 |
| Salt Creeks | 67 |
| Fledgling | 68 |
| Night Walk | 69 |

*Each that we lose takes part of us;*
*A crescent still abides,*
*Which like the moon, some turbid night,*
*Is summoned by the tides.*
—Emily Dickinson


*She followed slowly and she needed time,*
*as if something still were not surmounted;*
*and yet: as if, after a crossing over,*
*she would be done with walking, and would fly.*
—Rainer Maria Rilke

# Fledging

All summer a girl jumps
from the stone wall, legs
akimbo, arms
thrust in the air
for a split second

that indistinct moment
before slamming onto the macadam.

She waits each time
for her father to come
to see the smeared blood
and dirt, the tiny stones
embedded in her knees.

Each time she waits for him
to carry her to the house.

What he does not see:
how translucent her skin,
soft down that holds the light,
the promise of tiny wings,
and though she tries and tries
she can't yet fly.

# 1
# Night Lanterns

## At First There Was No Air

then an evening breeze kicked up,
turning wild, so while I
waited for the nurse
to clock the time of death,
wind tore through the house,
curtains billowing, branches
banging against the screens
like anger, unleashed,
or grief. Or what?

What happens
in those long moments
after the heart stops beating,
before the mind quiets?

It's all I could think,
sitting on the hall floor
waiting for her body to be moved,
not wanting to close the house,
so whatever force remained
could free itself.

The nurse packed and left,
my sister driven away,
finally, in a black car,
as she had been decades earlier
the summer she was sent to camp.

Back then I had watched
from the front steps, as the car
turned from the driveway
and disappeared. She was gone
all summer. It was hot and rainy,
but by fall she'd come home.

# It Begins

Clouds stretch

                         a sheer white

                 curtain across the sky.

She grows thin.

# Not This

The doctor reads from the chart

    *thickened tissue at the lung's base*

        as techs in green scrubs

  take her for another scan

return her shivering, no news

    or none they will share

        her milky eyes staring

  at her feet at the base of the bed

clubbed fingers the first sign

    we missed

        she says nothing this day or the next

  while we wait and whisper

open the curtains to the blue

      October sky season of birth

           season of death and whatever

   happened whatever damage

to her lungs—virus, toxin,

      bird droppings from the barn

         happened decades ago

in childhood.

# Alveoli

The word like a musical instrument,
    wood and strings playing Vivaldi
this Tuesday as we wait for the discharge nurse.

The CT scan shows scarring in the lungs,
    opaque spaces where alveoli, filled
with mucus, hardened to stone.

*Glassy lungs,* the nurse smiles, kindly,
    as he explains the scan, and for a moment
I see tumbled along the shoreline

the shards of white sea glass we treasured
    as kids, as if all along she's hidden them
secretly inside her.

# The Day Falling to Pieces

An envelope of medicine arrives, then another with oxygen tanks, rubber sheets, a wheelchair, which we hide, because we're not ready for this. By noon more meds, and we lose track of what needs to be kept cool, what to give her when, labeling and sorting pills into baskets. She asks for ham salad but the bread's stale, and we're out of juice. The oxygen tank, too close to the wall, overheats and shuts down. The kitchen fills with strangers—a hospice nurse, aide, a neighbor who walks in and suddenly looks scared, though not as scared as the rest of us. Phones keep ringing, a friend orders food for us, but *Can you please come pick it up?* Then the doorbell—two men with a hospital bed we said we didn't want. By 10 PM everyone's left, and we forgot to get Medihoney, and Cindy's stuck on the sofa, too weak to walk, too weak even to stand, and she needs to pee, so we lift her, drag her up three stairs to the wheelchair and wheel her to her bed. I don't know how to do this.

# Witness

I lie with her, my hand
covering hers, still warm,
still a pulse. Dusk seeps
into the room, shadows
the thin quilt that covers us.

I think back to our father,
home late, coming in
to say goodnight. He'd sit
on our bed, a dark silhouette
framed by a light in the hall:

*I've been working on the railroad*
he sings. He shows us a $100 bill.
We don't know what it means.
Some nights he tells us stories.
Other nights he plays his banjo.

Some nights in her sleep
my sister cries out.
Some nights he comes
to calm her. Some
to silence her.

# How to Ask

*what comes after:*
   *earth or fire?*
      *Fire.*

Then:

*Earth or sea or sky?*
    *Sea.*

And so it is.

# Sisters

I want to tell you the story
of our sad childhood, so you know
the fear you felt was real,
but you're sleeping, and your hands
are cold, so I tell you instead
the story of the nuns who came
each August to the shore, a dozen
or more, renting the yellow house
with the large screened porch.

Remember? We were young
and up early, sneaking to the beach
where each morning we'd find them
clapping like children as they
fed gulls or played tag,
running through sand in black
stockings and black shoes,
their long habits puffed
by wind, their veils floppy.

We learned from their joy,
that it comes unbidden
in a moment of surprise,
like your giggles
that shake you from sleep,
awake now long enough
for me to say goodnight.

# Morphine Drip

Her breathing eases, and I imagine

the drip as the strand of pearls

mother pulled from the dresser,

trusted to her small child-hands:

or rocks, shimmering and white,

collected to line the garden's edge;

white pins mapping hurricanes

or cross country drives;

thousands of miles,

thousands of streetlamps,

one by one, lighting her way.

# We Speak in Whispers

move in silence
from room to room, listen
to the oxygen's steady pump,

moisture bubbling through tubes.
Three days unresponsive. I sit
with her until someone else comes in.

Years from now I will remember
the counter scattered with crumbs
from half eaten sandwiches,

the tide low, winds calm,
cormorants perched motionless
in a line along the pilings. At first

they seem an omen, messengers
from the dead, but I will wonder later
if perhaps they were something other,

attendants in mourning or angels,
their black wings spread wide
against the sun's late day burn.

# Home Health Aide

She arrives when we are our saddest,
two suitcases and a carryall
on a bus from Virginia,
enough clothes to last until spring
if we're lucky. But we aren't.

Two days later we say goodbye
as she returns home, leaving us
to the dosings, the final hours
when we need her most,
not to care for Cindy, but to care

for us, shredded by grief
and fear and the awful unknown
in waiting for death.

# Snapper Blue

The nurse bathes her
props her against pillows
to ease her breathing
wraps her in a pink sweater
as though this afternoon
she will receive company.

I am dizzy with fear.
She should be lying down
but I am afraid to touch her
afraid to move her on my own
as if she will break into pieces.

So she dies sitting up
in a pink sweater
her jaw suddenly slack
mouth opening—last
sweet breaths of salt air—

like the snapper blues we caught
as kids, their tails smacking the dock
as we struggled to cut lines.

# Physician, Father

Smoke curled, rising
from the lid of a small green tin
where ashes from what looked like
tea leaves—atropine
or ephedra—smoldered.

Our mother, her shoulders
rounded, bent over the tin
inhaling smoke
to ease her wheezing.

To our father asthma
wasn't real disease,
only weakness,
so we learned to hide
our ills, to hide ourselves.

Even in the end my sister
refused all help, our father,
long dead, hovering so close
she could smell his Old Spice.

# Obituary

Cynthia, moon goddess, moon face, eyes cornflower blue. As a child, she kept a memory jar filled with shells she'd found, Mimi's gold thimble. Carried, too, in her back pocket night terrors, the spankings, wrapped her anger in silence, stuffed it up her sleeve. And this: hiding, glass breaking, her broken father who taught her the names of bones and how to saddle and mount a horse. Her horse, with whom she shared peppermints, bits from brunch. What she hated: seafood, pollen, pretense. What she feared: being seen. And what she loved: rock 'n roll, Joe, tinsel at Christmas. Glittered tissue in which she wrapped gifts. Charcoal sketches she'd made of her cat, the groundhogs by which she marked spring. Fall marked by the arrival of Royal terns. Her own birdies: beloved children and their children on her porch, their voices swelling inside her as dusk settled each night over the marsh. Golden hour of osprey returning to the rookery with fish. Constellations: Cassiopeia and Orion, undying light of heaven; shapes and stories of violence and vengeance, of loss and beauty she claimed as her own. Dry toast at 6 AM, late night TV. Darkness framed her life, but the deeper the darkness, the brighter pinpoints of light in the night sky: moonchild, luminous.

## Last Everything

Another day.
The bay deep blue
untidied with white caps,

the sky also blue and cloudless
as a late season flock
of common eiders flies south.

No last words,
or none any of us remember.
None of the usual markers either:

no murmuring or thirst,
no agitation—the desire to flee
the house or her own wrecked body—

no choking or gurgling, no fluids,
as though her body emptied itself
of everything but the stones in her lungs,

no whistling or rattling, just silence.
Silence, and finally a sigh,
and a few deep gulps of air as if

she'd been holding her breath all her life.

# Night Lanterns

We are here to spread her ashes,
the first cold day of fall,
six of us in a boat, while others
gather in small groups on the dock
beneath a sky streaked with pastels.

Just west of the island, we float
her paper urn where currents
carry it toward the salt creeks:
sage green, crusted
with Marsh Marigold, Rose
Mallow, wildflowers to seed
the space we once inhabited as kids.

We drift for a while,
and when the bay grows dark
head home for the usual family gathering,
the familiar stories suddenly held dear.

And late, return to the bay
with a dozen night lanterns,
those small hot air balloons we light,
waiting for the heat to build,
their thin paper walls as translucent
as her skin the last weeks of her life.

They sway and bobble along the beach
as though dancing to 50's music,
then one by one lift
into the dark, rising high
above the bay, lights flickering,
growing smaller and smaller
before vanishing
in the expanding darkness:

her burial ground, reaching
from the shoals of this island
deep into the sky above.

# 2
# Atlantic Flyway

# Ash, Snow

Embers crackle in the fire pit
and ashes caught in a breeze

swirl upward like the first
snow that will arrive this week

soft gray flakes
blanketing the earth.

# Deep Freeze

The bay freezes over.
Beneath its thin crust
my sister's ashes.

Her house stands empty

but a fox pair, tails curled
over them like coverlets,
huddles in the frigid noon sun
along the stone path
to her front steps.

# Bloom

A long winter
lately too much rain
a season since her death.

Now spring blooms
all at once.

I find her everywhere
in the paper thin
petals of the weeping
cherry, bleeding hearts
grown so lush
they crowd out the rose.

# Atlantic Flyway

A blitz of shore birds
flies north

where horseshoe crabs
spawn in the saltmarsh—

eggs buried in sand—
a buffet for red knots

ruddy turnstones
sanderlings her favorite.

# Fogbow

On the horizon
a fog gathers.

Look closely! Within it
a white rainbow,

ghostlike, rolling in.

# Squall

Ahead of the storm
a shelf cloud
races toward the beach
like a wave surging

its blue glow haunting:

torrents of rain (tears)
and wind (still) to come.

# Nocturne

Oh, Orb Weaver,
of course you are back.

It's nearly fall when you spin
your fragile webs

flexing each night high
in the corner of her porch

above the light
she always left on.

# Late Garden

Tossed from the dock,
the garden's last cuttings:
red zinnias, purple
dahlias, drawn
into the current,
floating, unhurried,
toward the wetlands.

A year ago at dusk.
A year ago. Dusk.

# Renewal

Grief flows in and out
like the tides

but today a storm
stalled along the coast

tore up the bay
left me breathless.

# After Ebb Tide

A widening path of silver
across the water glistens

as the moon rises
and a breeze takes hold

and the day gives way to evening
and the tide returns.

# Vespers

A red knot feeds
along the scrap line

and a heron, its black
silhouette against a yellow sky

watches over her ashes
still.

# 3
# Suddenly a Rush of Air

# In the Golden Hour, Cormorants

We noticed a cormorant,
black feathers and kinked neck,
a thin hooked bill, perched
on a piling facing the house as though
watching the oxygen tanks unloaded
from the back of a truck, the wheelchair
carried up the front stairs.

The next day there were more,
diving deep beneath the docks, feeding
for hours before coming to rest
one after another on pilings
until every one was taken.
A silent chorus, in their black robes,
and as the time shortened to a few days

they offered comfort—as long as they stayed
you wouldn't die, even as you refused
pudding, sweet tea, turned your face to the wall
as we moistened your lips with a wet cloth.

The last day was quiet, the water still
until your final breath when wind
suddenly kicked up. I watched
as they rose in unison, heading
south, ushering you away.

I wished them safe harbor.
I wish them safe return.

# Another Morning

Early, already humid,
the air salty. A dove
sunning itself on the deck,
dragonflies hovering
like memories:

our mother in the next room
angry with us both,
when suddenly a rush of air:
a great egret alights
in the bayberry, just feet from us,
its white feathers and wings
shimmering as a breeze
rustles the bush. For a moment
everything stops—
its beauty a grace note—
but you turn your back,
flushing the egret from its perch,
and walk away.

# Of Children

I'd wanted, for years, more children
but not in the way they finally came to me,
fully grown, sitting politely in a circle
as the bereavement counselor handed each
a pamphlet: *The Orphaned Adult.*

Worse was watching them
late morning leave for the funeral home.
They needed to do this on their own.
And I know: they aren't my children.
But their heartaches have become mine.

So too their joys. Tonight
Addison pulls me into the dark
to see the stars. She's five
and believes you are in the sky.

Some days I mistake a photo
I have of her walking the beach
with one of you at the same age,
light filled blue eyes, broad forehead,
your arm swinging a bucket of shells,
another sweet ordinary day.

# Here's the Thing

A surprise party your children planned,
baskets of fruit and pastries, September
daisies on tables beneath a white tent.

Grieving our mother's death
you closed yourself inside the house.
But we were all grieving.

When you finally showed up,
opened gifts, laughter echoing
across the bay, it was too late.

I understood the way you used silence
to shield yourself, and I, perhaps too eager
always to speak for you, for once didn't.

Not this time. I didn't tell you it was OK.
Your children hurt, too exhausted
even to say goodbye, your face burning

in the sun's glare as you looked
at tables stripped of linens,
ice from coolers melting into sand.

# Against Evanescence

In your silence, your lips sealed
as though stitched shut, you knew
I couldn't carry your fear or pain,
the struggle to breathe
or the late afternoon light
washing your room in shadows and gold.

I couldn't carry any of this.

But at least I tried
to carry the goodbyes for your children

who flew apart like sparrows
flushed from the crape myrtle
in the moments after your death,

or your friend who brought ginger cookies
an hour too late. To each

I offered some part of you, a story,
forbidden and likely half-true
from years of forgetting
and re-imagining.

I offered them your last words,
though there were none;
after all, how could you say goodbye,
and how can I, not wanting to forget
the shadows overtaking your room
as light faded, or how I fear
our stories re-imagined so often
will no longer hold you?

# Migration

Still, there is joy. Yesterday
I woke to the monarchs'
fall journey, the dune thick
with goldenrod, and everywhere
butterflies flitting from one
yellow plume to the next.

And last night, from the upstairs deck,
we watched Cygnus, 300 miles away,
launch from Wallops Island, a trail
of fire lifting in a perfect arc
through sky so crisp and clear,
the second stage so bright
the moon paled in comparison.

I am sad you weren't here to see it,
but I want to tell you
this morning gulls work the water
where a school of bluefish heads south,
and just beyond the breakers
two whales feed.

Even when you and I no longer are here
monarchs will reawaken and
venture north, laying eggs
in the milkweed, and a pair of osprey
will return to the buoy
where they have long nested,
where each night in darkness,
the Northern Cross rises overhead.

# 4
# Fledgling

# The Newest One at Three

Streetlamps.
A beach road at dusk.
On an upstairs porch
a party, a child
tasting cake, sweetness
she eagerly accepts as life.

# She's Going Out with the Tide

is what they said when the neighbor died,
is what they said when Mimi died,
though she was in the next room
beneath a white quilt.

I didn't notice the tide when my sister died.
But I check now and then to see
what's washing in, what's washing out,
keeping company with whoever has just left,

pulled by the moon, by currents
through foam and a shoal of broken shells,
pulled through deeper water,
to a deep seabed

of seamounts and lava,
canyons, and cold water seeps,
channels, the abyssal plain,
bones, minerals, memories, salt.

# Afterlife

The moon over the bay

      just before dawn. I wait

for the light to change,

      for the moon to fade,

disappear into blue. If only

      I could preserve

this moment, place it

      in a memory jar

with sea glass, a gold thimble.

      How else to remember a life?

Memory and its fragments

      always elusive,

even my grief, no matter

      the hold I have on it,

that, too, slipping away.

# Hymn to the Gods

God of Osprey and Egret,

    speckled eggs, bird calls;

God of pines and marsh,

    grasses bent by wind,

blue or gray or gold soaked skies,

    blue or gray or gold soaked bays;

God of mole crabs, cockles,

    terrapins resting in mud,

salt air, fish stink, coal tar

    blistered by sun; God

of summer squalls

    and lightening; God

of winter nights, Orion

      climbing skyward from the sea;

God of distant voices;

      God of memory and grief

and the mercy in this morning's

      breeze waking all she's left behind:

may its gentleness hold her.

# Sky Dance

As shadows spill across the bay at dusk
a quiet breeze, the time of day she loved
at summer's end, the crickets' song, their husks
like grief in drying grass, and high above
an osprey's circle dance. It soars
through swirls of milky blue and gray,
and hangs aloft. With drawn wings
swoops down and up again in play.
Soon it leaves its perch for winter grounds.
Does instinct hold some vestige of its mate,
delight or longing, momentary sounds
of whistles in the marsh that fall away?
On nights like this her presence feels alive,
her voice, the evening's lullaby.

## Salt Creeks

How old when we first sailed from the bay
    deep into the wetlands, pulling
the wooden dinghy onto shore?

At low tide eel grass pulsed in the currents,
    weaving itself through and around our legs.
We waded in tide pools,

clusters of moon snails and limpets
    anchored by the hundreds on rocks.
It seemed a place of wonder, the sun

taking hold, the shushing of marsh reeds,
    a hint of salt always in the air.
Only now do I think back

to how the air turned heavy
    and the sky dark as we returned
through the narrow inlet,

above us a commotion of wings,
    a duckling caught
in a gull's black beak,

where even now a heron
    with its great efficient height
stalks the mud flats close by.

# Fledgling

Feathers of wood thrush
and sparrow, her earrings fall
easily into the folds of her hair.

She seems still a child, eyelids
fluttering in sleep, her slow
waking this morning to a bird's

call, light casting its amber haze
over the down of her arm.
Soon new hair will grow.

Already a dozen or so dark
threads crisscross the pause
of skin between her legs.

In her feet, insistent
and wild, the wingbeat.

# Night Walk

a prism

    circles    a milk white

                moon

Cynthia

        her faint

  thin light.

# About the Author

Poet, teacher, and editor, Cheryl Baldi, is the author of *The Shapelessness of Water* (Kelsay Books, 2018) and a graduate of the Warren Wilson MFA Program for Writers. A former Pennsylvania Bucks County Poet Laureate, she was a finalist for the Frances Locke Memorial Poetry Award, and a 2023 Pushcart Prize nominee. She divides her time between coastal New Jersey and Bucks County where she volunteers for the Bucks County Poet Laureate Program and the Arts and Cultural Council.

www.ingramcontent.com/pod-product-compliance
Lightning Source LLC
Chambersburg PA
CBHW030914170426
43193CB00009BA/840